> "BE WHO GOD MEANT YOU TO BE AND YOU WILL SET THE WORLD ON FIRE."
> SAINT CATHERINE OF SIENA

T5-AQT-542

Middle School Girls, Grades 7th - 8th
Introducing a Bible Study Designed
Just for YOU!

Invite new and old friends to gather weekly for 20 weeks of engaging activities, stories, and fellowship.

We've prepared *everything* you'll need:

A LEADER'S CURRICULUM GUIDE

BLAZE KIT

Accompanying customized box filled with all the supplies you'll need for each week: Weekly Message Cards, **Prayer Journal**, T-Shirts and weekly gifts.

Additional Opportunities for Girls to Grow in Friendship with Christ:

DISCOVERING MY PURPOSE

Discover your Spiritual Gifts in a 7 week Bible study.

BETWEEN YOU & ME

A 40-day conversation guide for mothers and daughters.

walking with purpose

Visit us at walkingwithpurpose.com/BLAZE to help you get started today!

BLAZE
Prayer Journal

www.walkingwithpurpose.com

Authored by Lisa Brenninkmeyer
Cover design by Aliza Latta
Production management by Christine Welsko

IMPRIMATUR   + William E. Lori, S.T.D., Archbishop of Baltimore

The recommended Bible translations for use in Blaze and Walking with Purpose studies are: The New American Bible, which is the translation used in the United States for the readings at Mass; The Revised Standard Version, Catholic Edition; and The Jerusalem Bible.

Print: March 2018

ISBN: 978-1-943173-17-4

BLAZE Prayer Journal

Be who GOD meant you to be and you will set the world on fire.

ST CATHERINE of SIENA

blaze

4 Reasons to Use a Prayer Journal

1. Strengthens your friendship with God

A prayer journal is a way that you can connect with God, just like you were texting Him or sending Him a letter. You don't have to have a perfectly formulated prayer; you can just tell Him how you are and what you need.

2. Helps you organize your thoughts

There's something about just starting to write that can help get the jumble of thoughts entangled in your brain out on the paper. Writing your thoughts in a prayer journal instead of just mulling them over in your head reminds you that God is with you and cares about what you are going through.

3. Helps you bring your heart to God

God cares about and wants to hear about every single detail of your life. He is after your heart. None of your emotions are too big or too strong for Him. He wants to hear how you feel. Sometimes we don't know which emotions we're experiencing until we stop and try to write them down. Are you mad? Hurt? Sad? Excited? Worried? God wants you to come to Him honestly. He wants the real you.

4. Helps remind you that God comes through for you

After you've been keeping a prayer journal for a while, you'll realize that you have some recorded history with God. You can look back on things you've gone through, and see that God got you through it.

Today's Date:

Adoration

[This is where you thank God for WHO HE IS. This is different from WHAT HE GIVES. Examples: God is wise, loving, trustworthy, kind, strong, protective, gracious, forgiving, faithful, knows everything, sacrificing, holy, a good Father, faultless, loyal, sheltering, courageous]

Confession

[This is where you think about when you have been less than your best self. Remember, when we confess our sins, God ALWAYS forgives]

Thanksgiving

[This is where you thank God for what He has given you]

Supplication

[This is where you ask God for what you need]

Dear God,

Today I feel....

"Trust in the LORD with all your heart, on your own intelligence do not rely; in all your ways, be mindful of Him, and He will make straight your paths." Proverbs 3:5-6

Today's Date:

Adoration

Confession

Thanksgiving

Supplication

Dear God,

Today I feel....

"They that hope in the LORD will renew their strength, they will soar on eagles' wings; they will run and not grow weary, they will walk and not grow faint." Isaiah 40:31

Today's Date:

Adoration

Confession

Thanksgiving

Supplication

Dear God,

Today I feel....

"I command you: be strong and steadfast! Do not fear nor be dismayed, for the LORD, your God, is with you wherever you go." Joshua 1:9

Today's Date:

Adoration

Confession

Thanksgiving

Supplication

Dear God,

Today I feel....

"Blessed be the God and Father of our Lord Jesus Christ, the Father of compassion and God of all encouragement, who encourages us in our every affliction, so that we may be able to encourage those who are in any affliction with the encouragement with which we ourselves are encouraged by God." 2 Corinthians 1:3-4

Today's Date:

Adoration

Confession

Thanksgiving

Supplication

Dear God,

Today I feel....

"Peace I leave with you; My peace I give to you. Not as the world gives do I give it to you. Do not let your hearts be troubled or afraid." John 14:27

Today's Date:

Adoration

Confession

Thanksgiving

Supplication

Dear God,

Today I feel....

"God is our refuge and strength, a very present help in trouble." Psalm 46:1

Today's Date:

Adoration

Confession

Thanksgiving

Supplication

Dear God,

Today I feel....

"Therefore, encourage one another and build one another other up, as indeed you do." 1 Thessalonians 5:11

Today's Date:

Adoration

Confession

Thanksgiving

Supplication

Dear God,

Today I feel….

"When you pass through waters, I will be with you; through rivers, you shall not be swept away. When you walk through the fire, you will not be burned, nor will flames consume you." Isaiah 43:2

Today's Date:

Adoration

Confession

Thanksgiving

Supplication

Dear God,

Today I feel....

"Love the LORD, all you who are faithful to Him. The LORD protects the loyal, but repays the arrogant in full." Psalm 31:24

Today's Date:

Adoration

Confession

Thanksgiving

Supplication

Dear God,

Today I feel....

"But the LORD said to Samuel: Do not judge from his appearance or from his lofty stature, because I have rejected Him. God does not see as a mortal, who sees the appearance. The LORD looks into the heart." 1 Samuel 16:7

Today's Date:

Adoration

Confession

Thanksgiving

Supplication

Dear God,

Today I feel….

"For surely I know the plans I have for you, says the LORD, plans for welfare and not for harm, to give you a future with hope." Jeremiah 29:11

Today's Date:

Adoration

Confession

Thanksgiving

Supplication

Dear God,

Today I feel....

"I sought the LORD, and He answered me, delivered me from all my fears."
Psalm 34:5

Today's Date:

Adoration

Confession

Thanksgiving

Supplication

Dear God,

Today I feel....

"Blessed are the clean of heart, for they will see God." Matthew 5:8

Today's Date:

Adoration

Confession

Thanksgiving

Supplication

Dear God,

Today I feel....

"Finally, brothers, whatever is true, whatever is honorable, whatever is just, whatever is pure, whatever is lovely, whatever is gracious, if there is any excellence, and if there is anything worthy of praise, think about these things." Philippians 4:8

Today's Date:

Adoration

Confession

Thanksgiving

Supplication

Dear God,

Today I feel....

"I praise you, because I am wonderfully made; wonderful are your works! My very self you know." Psalm 139:14

Today's Date:

Adoration

Confession

Thanksgiving

Supplication

Dear God,

Today I feel….

"For we are His handiwork, created in Christ Jesus for good works that God has prepared in advance, that we should live in them." Ephesians 2:10

Today's Date:

Adoration

Confession

Thanksgiving

Supplication

Dear God,

Today I feel....

"God looked at everything that He had made, and found it very good. Evening came, and morning followed – the sixth day." Genesis 1:31

Today's Date:

Adoration

Confession

Thanksgiving

Supplication

Dear God,

Today I feel....

"Put on then, as God's chosen ones, holy and beloved, compassion, kindness, humility, gentleness, and patience." Colossians 3:12

Today's Date:

Adoration

Confession

Thanksgiving

Supplication

Dear God,

Today I feel....

"See what love the Father has bestowed on us that we may be the called children of God. Yet so we are. The reason the world does not know us is that it did not know Him." 1 John 3:1

Today's Date:

Adoration

Confession

Thanksgiving

Supplication

Dear God,

Today I feel....

"The LORD bless you and keep you! The LORD let His face shine upon you, and be gracious to you! The LORD look upon you kindly and give you peace!" Numbers 6:24-26

Today's Date:

Adoration

Confession

Thanksgiving

Supplication

Dear God,

Today I feel....

"I have told you this so that you might have peace in me. In this world you will have trouble, but take courage, I have conquered the world." John 16:33

Today's Date:

Adoration

Confession

Thanksgiving

Supplication

Dear God,

Today I feel....

"Bearing with one another and forgiving one another, if one has a grievance against another; as the Lord has forgiven you, so must you also do." Colossians 3:13

Today's Date:

Adoration

Confession

Thanksgiving

Supplication

Dear God,

Today I feel....

"With firm purpose you maintain peace; in peace, because of our trust in You."
Isaiah 26:3

Today's Date:

Adoration

Confession

Thanksgiving

Supplication

Dear God,

Today I feel….

"The patient are better than warriors, and those who rule their temper, better than the conqueror of a city." Proverbs 16:32

Today's Date:

Adoration

Confession

Thanksgiving

Supplication

Dear God,

Today I feel....

"The concern of the flesh is death, but the concern of the spirit is life and peace."
Romans 8:6

Today's Date:

Adoration

Confession

Thanksgiving

Supplication

Dear God,

Today I feel....

"For God so loved the world that he gave his only Son, so that everyone who believes
in Him might not perish but might have eternal life." John 3:16

Today's Date:

Adoration

Confession

Thanksgiving

Supplication

Dear God,

Today I feel....

"For I am convinced that neither death, nor life, nor angels, nor principalities, nor present things, nor future things, nor powers, nor height, nor depth, nor any other creature will be able to separate us from the love of God in Christ Jesus our Lord." Romans 8:38-39

Today's Date:

Adoration

Confession

Thanksgiving

Supplication

Dear God,

Today I feel....

"Beloved, let us love one another, because love is of God; everyone who loves is begotten by God and knows God." 1 John 4:7

Today's Date:

Adoration

Confession

Thanksgiving

Supplication

Dear God,

Today I feel....

"God loves each of us as if there were only one of us." -Saint Augustine

Today's Date:

Adoration

Confession

Thanksgiving

Supplication

Dear God,

Today I feel....

"Indeed, the word of God is living and effective, sharper than any two-edged sword, penetrating even between soul and spirit, joints and marrow, and able to discern reflections and thoughts of the heart." Hebrews 4:12

Today's Date:

Adoration

Confession

Thanksgiving

Supplication

Dear God,

Today I feel....

"Be strong and steadfast; have no fear or dread of them, for it is the LORD, your God, who marches with you; He will never fail you or forsake you." Deuteronomy 31:6

Today's Date:

Adoration

Confession

Thanksgiving

Supplication

Dear God,

Today I feel....

"Commit your way to the LORD; trust in Him, and He will act." Psalm 37:5

Today's Date:

Adoration

Confession

Thanksgiving

Supplication

Dear God,

Today I feel....

"Jesus looked at them and said, 'For human beings this is impossible, but for God all things are possible.'" Matthew 19:26

Today's Date:

Adoration

Confession

Thanksgiving

Supplication

Dear God,

Today I feel....

"All Scripture is inspired by God and is useful for teaching, for refutation, for correction, and for training in righteousness, so that one who belongs to God may be competent, equipped for every good work." 2 Timothy 3:16-17

Today's Date:

Adoration

Confession

Thanksgiving

Supplication

Dear God,

Today I feel....

"I can do all things through Him who strengthens me." Philippians 4:13

Today's Date:

Adoration

Confession

Thanksgiving

Supplication

Dear God,

Today I feel....

"Whatever you do, do from the heart, as for the Lord and not for others, knowing that you will receive from the Lord the due payment of the inheritance; be slaves of the Lord Christ." Colossians 3:23-24

Today's Date:

Adoration

Confession

Thanksgiving

Supplication

Dear God,

Today I feel….

"Let no one have contempt for your youth, but set an example for those who believe, in speech, conduct, love, faith, and purity." 1 Timothy 4:12

Today's Date:

Adoration

Confession

Thanksgiving

Supplication

Dear God,

Today I feel....

"Therefore, since we are surrounded by so great a cloud of witnesses, let us also rid ourselves of every burden and sin that clings to us and persevere in running the race that lies before us." Hebrews 12:1

Today's Date:

Adoration

Confession

Thanksgiving

Supplication

Dear God,

Today I feel....

"Do nothing out of selfishness or out of vainglory; rather, humbly regard others as more important than yourselves." Philippians 2:3

Today's Date:

Adoration

Confession

Thanksgiving

Supplication

Dear God,

Today I feel....

"No trial has come to you but what is human. God is faithful and will not let you be tried beyond your strength; but with the trial He will also provide a way out, so that you may be able to bear it." 1 Corinthians 10:13

Today's Date:

Adoration

Confession

Thanksgiving

Supplication

Dear God,

Today I feel….

"The LORD is my light and my salvation; whom shall I fear? The LORD is my life's refuge; of whom should I be afraid?" Psalm 27:1

Today's Date:

Adoration

Confession

Thanksgiving

Supplication

Dear God,

Today I feel....

"He said to them, "Because of your little faith. Amen, I say to you, if you have faith the size of a mustard seed, you will say to this mountain, 'Move from here to there,' and it will move. Nothing will be impossible for you." Matthew 17:20

Today's Date:

Adoration

Confession

Thanksgiving

Supplication

Dear God,

Today I feel....

"Even though I walk through the valley of the shadow of death, I will fear no evil, for You are with me; Your rod and Your staff comfort me." Psalm 23:4

Today's Date:

Adoration

Confession

Thanksgiving

Supplication

Dear God,

Today I feel....

"This is my commandment: that you love one another as I love you. No one has greater love than this, to lay down one's life for one's friends." John 15:12-13

Today's Date:

Adoration

Confession

Thanksgiving

Supplication

Dear God,

Today I feel....

"Walk with the wise and you become wise, but the companion of fools fares badly."
Proverbs 13:20

Today's Date:

Adoration

Confession

Thanksgiving

Supplication

Dear God,

Today I feel….

"Do to others as you would have them do to you." Luke 6:31

Today's Date:

Adoration

Confession

Thanksgiving

Supplication

Dear God,

Today I feel….

"A friend is a friend at all times, and a brother is born for the time of adversity."
Proverbs 17:17

Today's Date:

Adoration

Confession

Thanksgiving

Supplication

Dear God,

Today I feel....

"Listen to counsel and receive instruction, that you may eventually become wise."
Proverbs 19:20

Today's Date:

Adoration

Confession

Thanksgiving

Supplication

Dear God,

Today I feel….

"Rejoice in hope, endure in affliction, persevere in prayer." Romans 12:12

Today's Date:

Adoration

Confession

Thanksgiving

Supplication

Dear God,

Today I feel….

"May the God of hope fill you with all joy and peace in believing, so that you may abound in hope by the power of the Holy Spirit." Romans 15:13

Today's Date:

Adoration

Confession

Thanksgiving

Supplication

Dear God,

Today I feel....

"This is the day that the LORD has made; let us rejoice in it and be glad."
Psalm 118:24

Today's Date:

Adoration

Confession

Thanksgiving

Supplication

Dear God,

Today I feel....

"Be who God meant you to be and you will set the world on fire."
-Saint Catherine of Siena

Today's Date:

Adoration

Confession

Thanksgiving

Supplication

Dear God,

Today I feel....

"We destroy arguments and every pretension raising itself against the knowledge of God, and take every thought captive in obedience of Christ." 2 Corinthians 10:5

Today's Date:

Adoration

Confession

Thanksgiving

Supplication

Dear God,

Today I feel....

"The truth is the truth even if no one believes it, and a lie is a lie even if everyone believes it." –Venerable Fulton Sheen

Today's Date:

Adoration

Confession

Thanksgiving

Supplication

Dear God,

Today I feel....

"Then you will know the truth, and the truth will set you free." John 8:32

Today's Date:

Adoration

Confession

Thanksgiving

Supplication

Dear God,

Today I feel....

"Do not accept anything as the truth if it lacks love. And do not accept anything as love which lacks truth." -Saint Edith Stein

Today's Date:

Adoration

Confession

Thanksgiving

Supplication

Dear God,

Today I feel....

"The LORD your God is in your midst, a mighty savior, who will rejoice over you with gladness, and renew you in His love, who will sing joyfully because of you." Zephaniah 3:17

Today's Date:

Adoration

Confession

Thanksgiving

Supplication

Dear God,

Today I feel....

"Let your life be free from love of money but be content with what you have, for He has said, 'I will never forsake you or abandon you.'" Hebrews 13:5

Today's Date:

Adoration

Confession

Thanksgiving

Supplication

Dear God,

Today I feel....

"LORD, You are good and forgiving, most merciful to all who call on You."
Psalm 86:5

Today's Date:

Adoration

Confession

Thanksgiving

Supplication

Dear God,

Today I feel....

"From afar the LORD appears: with age-old love I have loved You; so I have kept my mercy toward You." Jeremiah 31:3

Today's Date:

Adoration

Confession

Thanksgiving

Supplication

Dear God,

Today I feel....

"Since love grows within you, so beauty grows. For love is the beauty of the soul."
-Saint Augustine

Today's Date:

Adoration

Confession

Thanksgiving

Supplication

Dear God,

Today I feel....

"No foul language should come out of your mouths, but only such as is good for needed edification, that it may impart grace to those who hear." Ephesians 4:29

Today's Date:

Adoration

Confession

Thanksgiving

Supplication

Dear God,

Today I feel....

"Kind words can be short and easy to speak, but their echoes are truly endless."
-Saint Teresa of Calcutta

Today's Date:

Adoration

Confession

Thanksgiving

Supplication

Dear God,

Today I feel....

"Behold, I stand at the door and knock. If anyone hears My voice and opens the door, (then) I will enter his house and dine with him, and he with Me." Revelation 3:20

Today's Date:

Adoration

Confession

Thanksgiving

Supplication

Dear God,

Today I feel....

"God loves each one of us as if there were only one of us." -Saint Augustine

Today's Date:

Adoration

Confession

Thanksgiving

Supplication

Dear God,

Today I feel....

"In the evening of my life I shall appear before You with empty hands, for I do not ask You to count my works. All our justices are stained in Your eyes. I want therefore to clothe myself in Your own justice and receive from Your love the eternal possession of Yourself." -Saint Therese of Lisieux

Today's Date:

Adoration

Confession

Thanksgiving

Supplication

Dear God,

Today I feel....

Speak the truth, even if your voice shakes. -Anonymous

Today's Date:

Adoration

Confession

Thanksgiving

Supplication

Dear God,

Today I feel....

"Ignorance of Scripture is ignorance of Christ." -Saint Jerome

Today's Date:

Adoration

Confession

Thanksgiving

Supplication

Dear God,

Today I feel....

"Your word is a lamp to my feet, a light for my path." Psalm 119:105

Today's Date:

Adoration

Confession

Thanksgiving

Supplication

Dear God,

Today I feel....

"Our hearts were made for You, O Lord, and they are restless until they rest in You."
-Saint Augustine

Today's Date:

Adoration

Confession

Thanksgiving

Supplication

Dear God,

Today I feel….

"Find your delight in the LORD who will give you your heart's desire." Psalm 37:4

Today's Date:

Adoration

Confession

Thanksgiving

Supplication

Dear God,

Today I feel....

"Love God, serve God; everything is in that." -Saint Clare of Assisi

Today's Date:

Adoration

Confession

Thanksgiving

Supplication

Dear God,

Today I feel....

"Do not conform yourselves to this age but be transformed by the renewal of your mind, that you may discern what is the will of God, what is good and pleasing and perfect." Romans 12:2

Today's Date:

Adoration

Confession

Thanksgiving

Supplication

Dear God,

Today I feel....

"For by grace you have been saved through faith, and this is not from you; it is the gift of God." Ephesians 2:8

Today's Date:

Adoration

Confession

Thanksgiving

Supplication

Dear God,

Today I feel....

"A thief comes only to steal and slaughter and destroy; I came so that they may might have life and have it more abundantly." John 10:10

Today's Date:

Adoration

Confession

Thanksgiving

Supplication

Dear God,

Today I feel....

"In contrast, the fruit of the Spirit is love, joy, peace, patience, kindness, generosity, faithfulness." Galatians 5:22

Today's Date:

Adoration

Confession

Thanksgiving

Supplication

Dear God,

Today I feel….

"If we acknowledge our sins, He is faithful and just and will forgive us our sins and cleanse us from every wrongdoing." 1 John 1:9

Today's Date:

Adoration

Confession

Thanksgiving

Supplication

Dear God,

Today I feel....

"Jesus said to him, 'I am the way and the truth and the life. No one comes to the Father except through Me.'" John 14:6

Today's Date:

Adoration

Confession

Thanksgiving

Supplication

Dear God,

Today I feel....

"But seek first His kingdom [of God] and His righteousness, and all these things will be given you besides." Matthew 6:33

Today's Date:

Adoration

Confession

Thanksgiving

Supplication

Dear God,

Today I feel....

"Cast all your worries on Him because He cares for you." 1 Peter 5:7

Today's Date:

Adoration

Confession

Thanksgiving

Supplication

Dear God,

Today I feel....

"Come to Me, all you who labor and are burdened, and I will give you rest."
Matthew 11:28

Today's Date:

Adoration

Confession

Thanksgiving

Supplication

Dear God,

Today I feel....

"So whoever is in Christ is a new creation: the old things have passed away; behold, new things have come." 2 Corinthians 5:17

Today's Date:

Adoration

Confession

Thanksgiving

Supplication

Dear God,

Today I feel....

"But He said to me, 'My grace is sufficient for you, for power is made perfect in weakness.' I will rather boast most gladly of my weaknesses, in order that the power of Christ may dwell with me." 2 Corinthians 12:9

Today's Date:

Adoration

Confession

Thanksgiving

Supplication

Dear God,

Today I feel....

"For, if you confess with your mouth that Jesus is Lord and believe in your heart that God raised Him from the dead, you will be saved." Romans 10:9

85

Today's Date:

Adoration

Confession

Thanksgiving

Supplication

Dear God,

Today I feel....

"But without faith it is impossible to please Him, for anyone who approaches God must believe that He exists and that He rewards those who seek Him." Hebrews 11:6

Today's Date:

Adoration

Confession

Thanksgiving

Supplication

Dear God,

Today I feel....

"You have been told, O Mortal, what is good, and what the LORD requires of you: Only to do justice and to love goodness, and to walk humbly with your God." Micah 6:8

Today's Date:

Adoration

Confession

Thanksgiving

Supplication

Dear God,

Today I feel....

"So let us confidently approach the throne of grace to receive mercy and to find grace for timely help." Hebrews 4:16

Today's Date:

Adoration

Confession

Thanksgiving

Supplication

Dear God,

Today I feel....

"There is no salvation through anyone else, nor is there is any other name under heaven given to the human race by which we must be saved." Acts 4:12

Today's Date:

Adoration

Confession

Thanksgiving

Supplication

Dear God,

Today I feel....

"Just so, your light must shine before others, that they may see your good deeds and glorify your heavenly Father." Matthew 5:16

Today's Date:

Adoration

Confession

Thanksgiving

Supplication

Dear God,

Today I feel....

"I fear nothing for God is with me." -Saint Joan of Arc

Today's Date:

Adoration

Confession

Thanksgiving

Supplication

Dear God,

Today I feel....

"Nothing created has ever been able to fill the heart of man. God alone can fill it infinitely." -Saint Thomas Aquinas

Today's Date:

Adoration

Confession

Thanksgiving

Supplication

Dear God,

Today I feel....

"You are not defeated until the moment you quit." -Father Mike Schmitz

Today's Date:

Adoration

Confession

Thanksgiving

Supplication

Dear God,

Today I feel....

"It doesn't take much time to become a saint, only much love."
-Venerable Fulton Sheen

Today's Date:

Adoration

Confession

Thanksgiving

Supplication

Dear God,

Today I feel….

"You pay God a great compliment by asking great things of Him."
-Saint Teresa of Avila

Today's Date:

Adoration

Confession

Thanksgiving

Supplication

Dear God,

Today I feel….

"Happy Girls are the prettiest." -Audrey Hepburn

Today's Date:

Adoration

Confession

Thanksgiving

Supplication

Dear God,

Today I feel....

"The love of God is not generic. God looks with love upon every man and woman, calling them by NAME." -Pope Francis

Today's Date:

Adoration

Confession

Thanksgiving

Supplication

Dear God,

Today I feel….

"It is better to be the child of God than the king of the whole world."
-Saint Aloysius Gonzaga

Today's Date:

Adoration

Confession

Thanksgiving

Supplication

Dear God,

Today I feel….

"Remember, the sinner who is sorry for his sins is closer to God than the just man who boasts of his good works." -Saint Padre Pio

Today's Date:

Adoration

Confession

Thanksgiving

Supplication

Dear God,

Today I feel....

"Begin now to be what you will be hereafter." -Saint Jerome

Today's Date:

Adoration

Confession

Thanksgiving

Supplication

Dear God,

Today I feel....

"What can we do to keep our heart from going numb? Go forth and proclaim the joy of the gospel." -Pope Francis

NOTES

NOTES

NOTES

NOTES